CIENCIAS NATURALES 1º ESO
PROYECTO BILINGÜE WORKBOOK TWO

1ª Edición: febrero de 2008

Composición de portada: Lulu.com

Maquetación: Francisco José Martínez Ruiz

Editor: Lulu.com

Lulu Enterprises
26-28 Hammersmith Grove
London W6 7BA

www.lulu.com

ISBN: 978-1-84799-616-9

CIENCIAS NATURALES 1º ESO
PROYECTO BILINGÜE WORKBOOK TWO

María Mercedes Bautista Arnedo

Licenciada en Ciencias Biológicas

Prólogo

La enseñanza bilingüe de las ciencias naturales supone para muchos de los profesores que se inician, un verdadero reto, ya que significa hacer frente a problemas de muy diversa naturaleza en lo concerniente a aspectos metodológicos, de contenido, lengua y búsqueda de materiales. El material didáctico se convierte en un problema para el profesor. Se suele optar por la adaptación del material existente en español o por la incorporación de material en lengua extranjera procedente del país de origen.

Resulta relativamente sencillo encontrar materiales didácticos de ciencias de la naturaleza en inglés. Sin embargo, en la mayoría de los casos, no son apropiados para su uso en la clase, ya que los textos en la lengua original poseen un nivel demasiado elevado para nuestros estudiantes en lengua extranjera. Por esta razón, el profesor necesita trabajar en la adaptación de estos materiales al nivel que tienen los estudiantes del idioma inglés.

Con estos materiales se proporciona al profesorado que imparta enseñanzas bilingües, un material útil y concreto en inglés, y una herramienta que permita una autoformación para impartir tópicos de ciencias naturales a un nivel lingüístico elemental en inglés, y que además les posibilite guiar al alumnado de forma clara, concisa y fácilmente entendible para el mismo.

Estos materiales están orientados para ser utilizados en un programa bilingüe para introducir contenidos de Ciencias Naturales a nivel de 1º de ESO, dentro del Plan para el Fomento del Plurilingüísmo de la Junta de Andalucía.

En **CIENCIAS NATURALES 1º ESO PROYECTO BILINGÜE WORKBOOK TWO** se recogen actividades para trabajar los contenidos relacionados con el **Bloque "Los materiales terrestres"** propuestos para la materia de Ciencias de la Naturaleza de 1º de ESO en el Real Decreto 1631/2006, por el que se establecen las enseñanzas mínimas correspondientes a la Educación Secundaria Obligatoria.

María Mercedes Bautista Arnedo

INDICE DE CONTENIDOS

Unit I

1. THE ATMOSPHERE: GAS IN EARTH

ACTIVITIES

1) Lecture: PARTS OF THE EARTH " THE ATMOSPHERE"

On the surface of the Earth, there are three different parts.

- The atmosphere
- The hydrosphere
- The lithosphere

The atmosphere is the gaseous layer that surrounds the Earth. It is formed by air, water, dust, etc. Life is impossible without atmosphere.

The atmosphere has **several layers,** but the most important ones are the troposphere and the stratosphere because the air is there.

- The **TROPOSPHERE.** It is the **closest layer to the Earth's surface.** It can be 15 km high. The weather phenomena (the rain, the wind, the snow, etc) take place in this layer.

- The **STRATOSPHERE.** This layer can be 50 km high. **Ozone is in this layer.** Ozone is a variety of oxygen, and it is a solar protector because it eliminates the dangerous radiations of the Sun.

2) Look.

Look at this photo of the Earth.

- What do clouds look like from space?

- Can we see the atmosphere?

3) Read. What is the atmosphere?

The **atmosphere** is the **air** which surrounds the Earth.

Air is a mixture of gases. It is mainly **nitrogen** and **oxygen**. There are also small quantities of **carbon dioxide**, **ozone** and **water vapour**.

The atmosphere is essential to life on Earth:

- It has the oxygen which all living things breathe. It also has carbon dioxide which plants need for photosynthesis.
- Carbon dioxide and other gases are like a blanket which retains the Earth's heat.
- Ozone filters harmful ultraviolet rays.

4) Read. The layers of the atmosphere.

The **troposphere** is the lowest layer.

- Most gases are in this layer.
- Plants and animals live in the troposphere.

The **stratosphere** is the next layer.

There is a thin layer of ozone in the upper stratosphere. This is called the **ozone layer.** This is called the **ozone layer.**

As we travel higher, the gases become less dense In **outer space** there is no atmosphere.

5) Read. Weather phenomena.

The principal weather phenomena are precipitation and wind.

Precipitation is water, such as rain, snow or hail, which falls from the atmosphere to the Earth.

Wind is the movement of air, and has different names depending on how strongly it blows. Breezes are gentle winds. Hurricanes are violent winds.

6) Complete the sentences.

The air which surrounds the Earth contains five gases: ....

The atmosphere has three layers:...........................

7) Label the Earth's Atmosphere.

Label the **layers of the Earth's** atmosphere using the terms:

Exosphere: the outermost layer of the Earth's atmosphere, where atmospheric pressure and temperature are low.

Ionosphere: the atmospheric layer between the mesosphere and the exosphere; it is part of the thermosphere.

Mesosphere: the atmospheric layer between the stratosphere and the ionosphere.

Stratosphere: the atmospheric layer between the troposphere and the mesosphere. The stratosphere is characterized by a slight temperature increase with altitude and by the absence of clouds.

Thermosphere: the layer of the atmosphere located above part of the ionosphere (starting at the coldest part of the atmosphere) and below outer space; it consists of the exosphere and part of the ionosphere.

Troposphere: the lowest layer of the Earth's atmosphere. The weather and clouds occur in the troposphere.

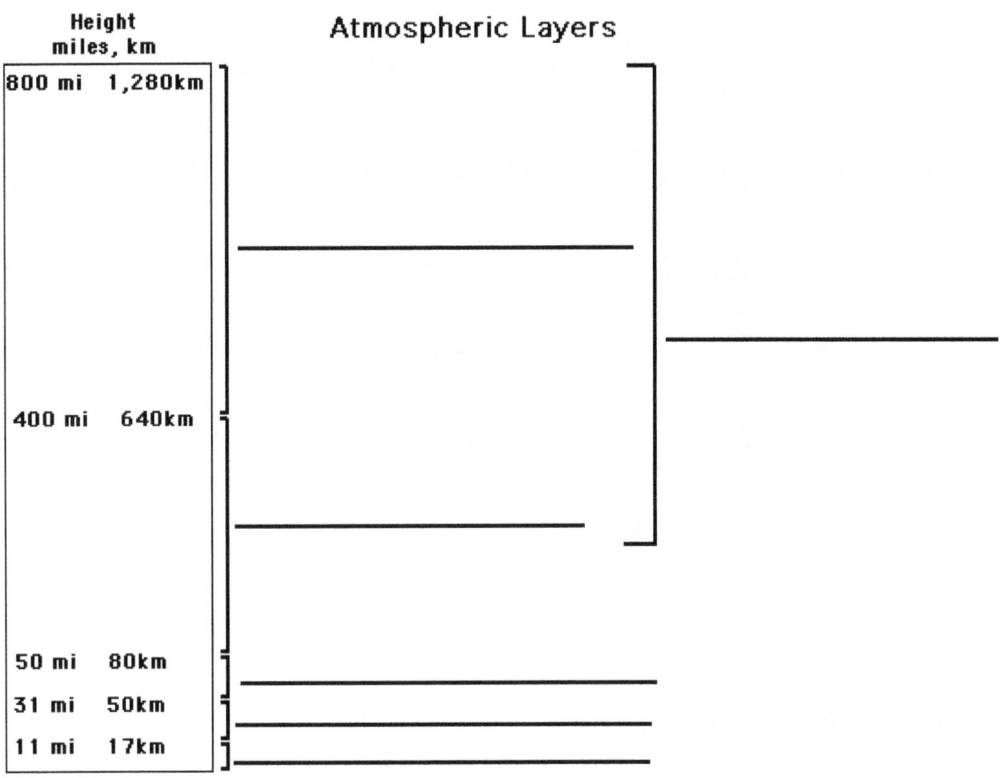

8) Choose the right option.

The percentages of the gases in the atmosphere today are:

- ❑ 10% Nitrogen, 50% Oxygen, 40% Carbon Dioxide
- ❑ 20% Nitrogen, 70% Oxygen, 10% Carbon Dioxide
- ❑ 58% Nitrogen, 31% Oxygen, 11% Argon
- ❑ 78% Nitrogen, 21% Oxygen, 1% Argon

9) Choose the right option.

A hole in the ozone layer increases the risk of:

- ❑ Global warming
- ❑ Global freezing
- ❑ Skin cancer
- ❑ Chicken pox

10) What is the Temperature? Complete the sentences using the most correct temperature word from the box.

cold	hot	warm	cool	chilly

1. It is *freezing* outside.

2. It is__________ today.

3. It was___________ yesterday

4. It is____________ outside.

5. It was_____________ yesterday.

11) How to Measure Air Temperature.

- We use a **thermometer** to measure how HOT or COLD it is outside. This measurement is known as the **temperature!**
- Thermometers can help you decide what to wear before going outside.
- **Record** the temperature for two weeks and see how the temperature can change every day!

1. **Put** the thermometer in a place that is not too sunny or too shady.
2. **Check** and **record** the temperature at least **three times (3x)** a day (once in the **morning**, once in the **afternoon**, and once in the **evening**).
3. **Place** a **small dot** on the chart to represent the temperature for each day and **record** the time you measured the temperature. (See example below).
4. At the end of each day, <u>draw a line</u> to connect the dots. (See example below).
5. Record the <u>highest</u> and <u>lowest</u> temperature for each day. (See example below).

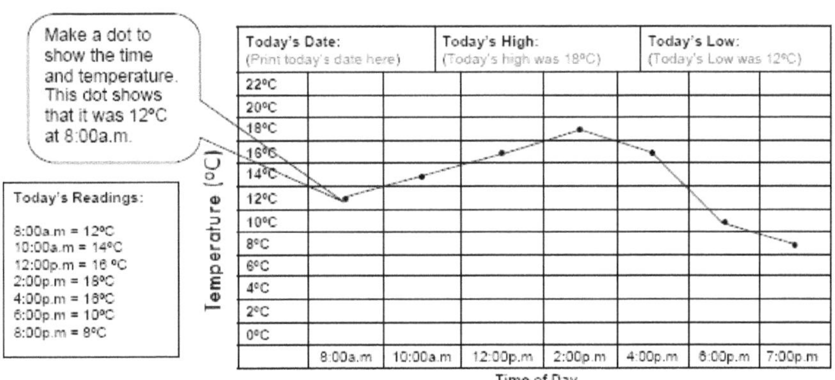

12) Join with arrows. Prepare for the Weather.

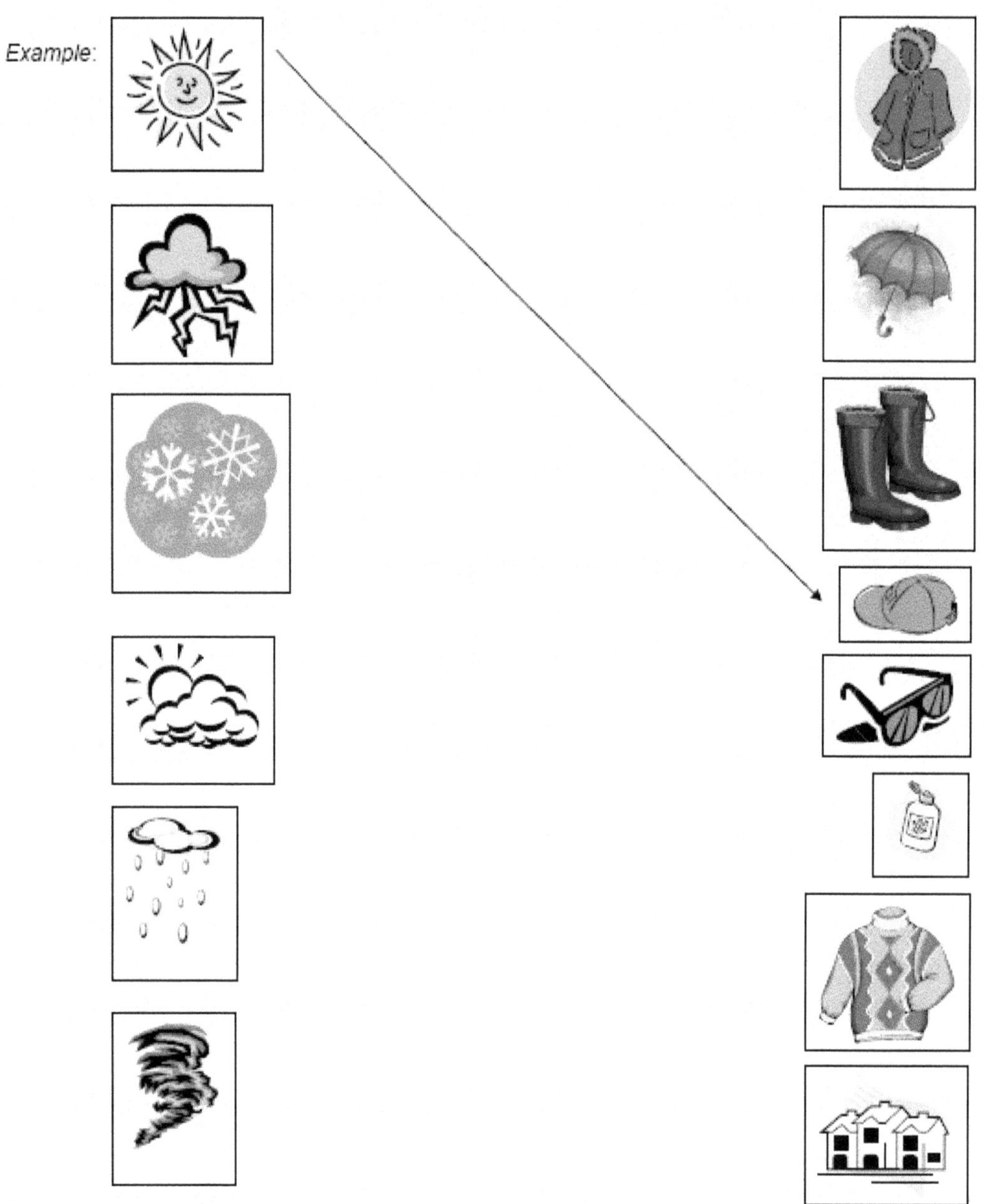

13) Join with arrows. How's the weather? (I)

It's cloudy

It's snowy

It's windy

It's sunny

It's rainy

14) Join with arrows. How's the weather? (II)

It's warm

It's cool

It's hot

It's foggy

It's cold

It's stormy

15) Layers of Earth's Atmosphere.

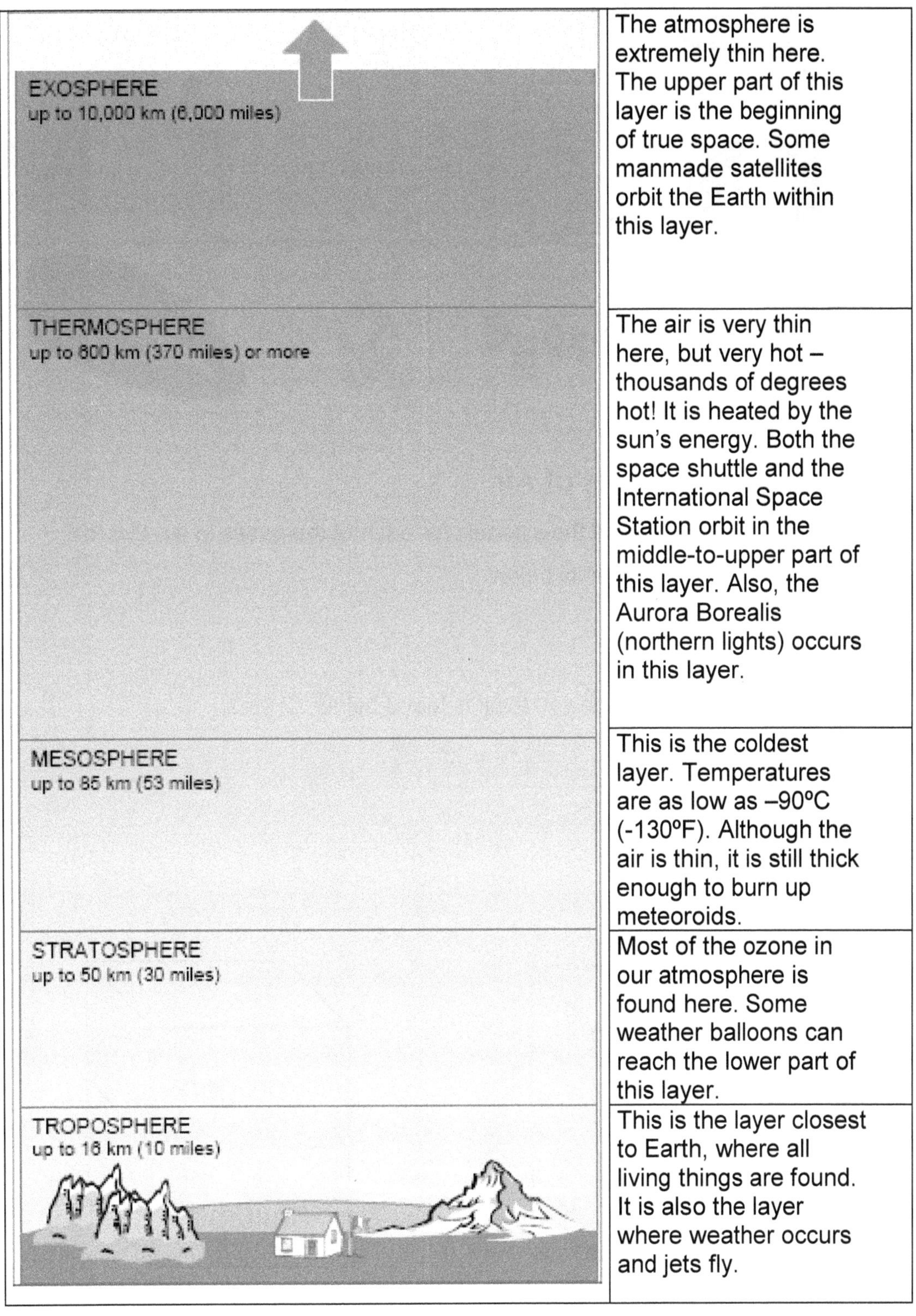

EXOSPHERE up to 10,000 km (6,000 miles)	The atmosphere is extremely thin here. The upper part of this layer is the beginning of true space. Some manmade satellites orbit the Earth within this layer.
THERMOSPHERE up to 600 km (370 miles) or more	The air is very thin here, but very hot – thousands of degrees hot! It is heated by the sun's energy. Both the space shuttle and the International Space Station orbit in the middle-to-upper part of this layer. Also, the Aurora Borealis (northern lights) occurs in this layer.
MESOSPHERE up to 85 km (53 miles)	This is the coldest layer. Temperatures are as low as –90°C (-130°F). Although the air is thin, it is still thick enough to burn up meteoroids.
STRATOSPHERE up to 50 km (30 miles)	Most of the ozone in our atmosphere is found here. Some weather balloons can reach the lower part of this layer.
TROPOSPHERE up to 16 km (10 miles)	This is the layer closest to Earth, where all living things are found. It is also the layer where weather occurs and jets fly.

Put these pictures into the correct layer of the atmosphere.

16) Main Ingredients of Air.

a) Use a periodic table to find the symbols for each of the gases in air. List the ingredients and write the symbol below.

b) Which composition of air do you think is found below 72 km?

Above 800 km?

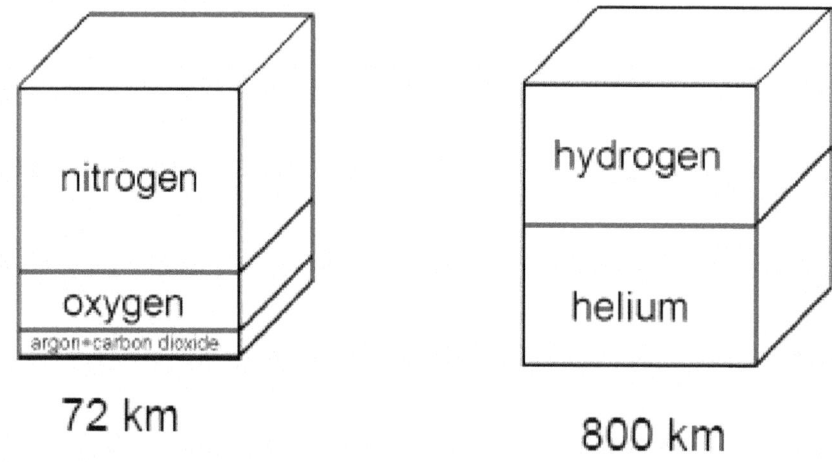

17) **Match the weather words and pictures.**

18) **Match the weather to the seasons.**

19) **Find the weather words!**

20) Cloud Key.

- Cut out the wheel.
- Cut out the two shaded areas inside the wheel.
- This is the top wheel of your cloud key.

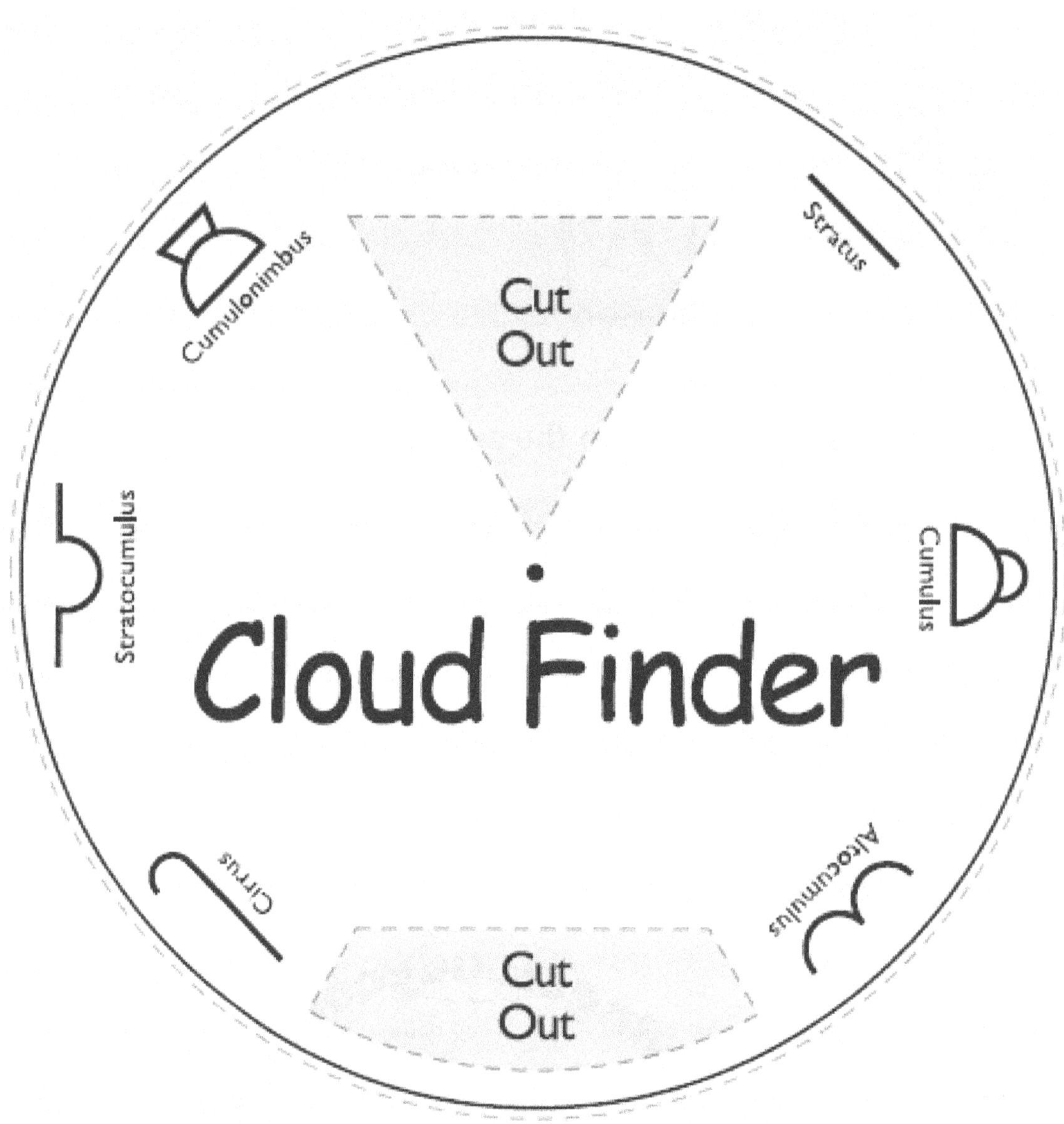

21) Watching the weather quiz.

Complete the sentences (Use the words in the box).

air pressure	temperature	precipitation	wind speed
satellite	radar	wind direction	

a) A thermometer measures ....

b) A barometer measures ....

c) A rain gauge measures ....

d) A weather vane measures ....

e) An anemometer measures ....

f) A ....takes pictures of clouds from space.

g) A .... shows where and how much rain is falling.

22) **Join with arrows.**

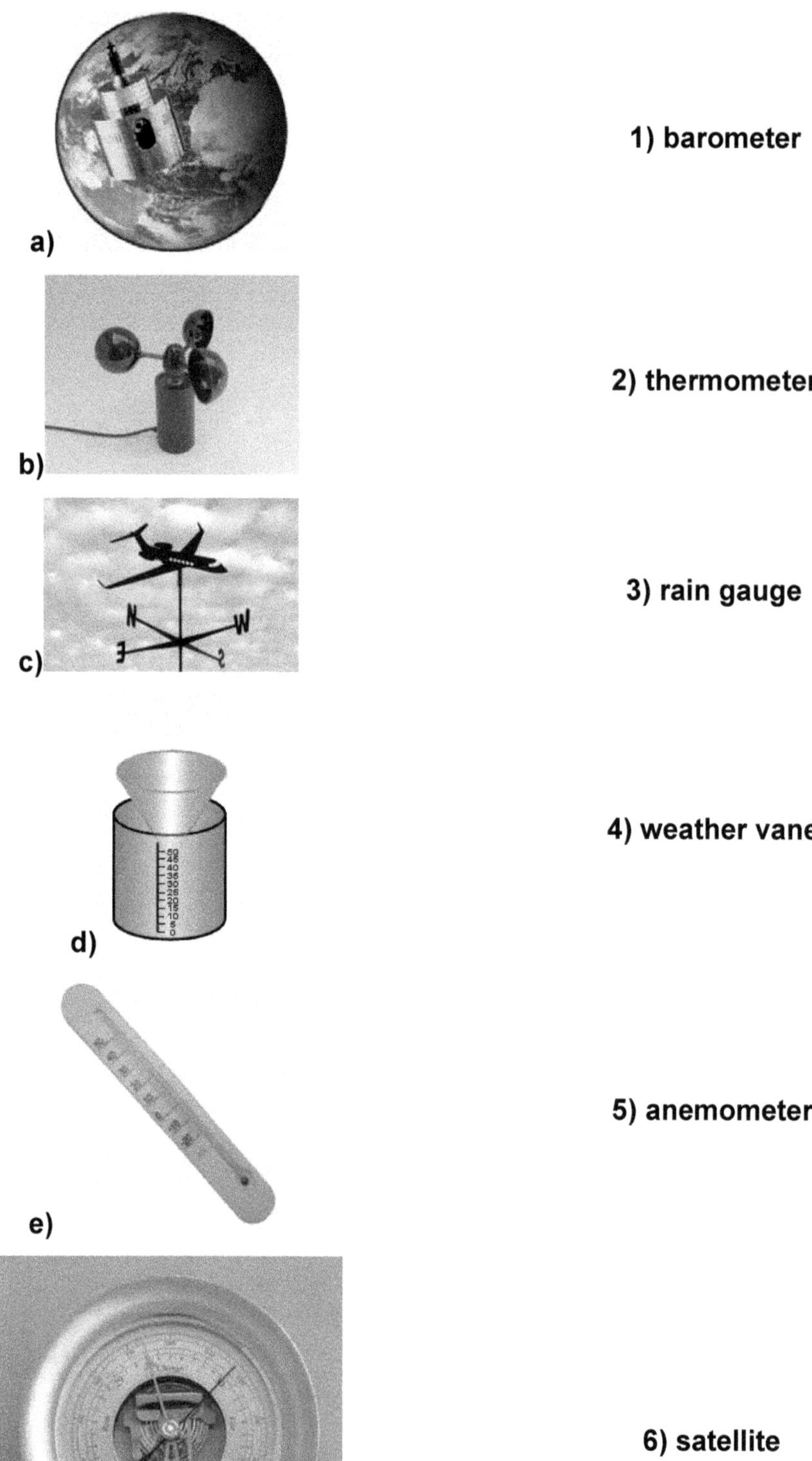

1) barometer

2) thermometer

3) rain gauge

4) weather vane

5) anemometer

6) satellite

23) What Types of Clouds Can You Find in the Sky?

Scientists classify clouds into three main categories - stratus, cumulus, and stratus. In this activity you will observe and learn how to identify these three types of clouds and the type of weather they bring.

- **Stratus clouds** are low, flat, gray clouds that look like sheets covering the sky. They are the closest clouds to the ground. They can produce rain, drizzle, or mist.

- **Cumulus clouds** are puffy and white like cotton balls. They usually indicate fair weather. Sometimes they grow very large and become thunderheads. As these clouds gather they create thunder and lightning and produce precipitation in the form of rain and hail.

- **Cirrus clouds** are thin, curly, wispy clouds. They are high in the atmosphere that the water droplets freeze into ice crystals. They often indicate an incoming storm or weather change.

24) Observe seasonal changes in the amount of sunlight reaching locations on Earth.

http://www.classzone.com/books/earth_science/terc/content/visualizations/es1704/es1704page01.cfm

25) Observe an animation of land and sea breezes.

http://www.classzone.com/books/earth_science/terc/content/visualizations/es1903/es1903page01.cfm

26) Compare and contrast warm and cold fronts.

http://www.classzone.com/books/earth_science/terc/content/visualizations/es2002/es2002page01.cfm

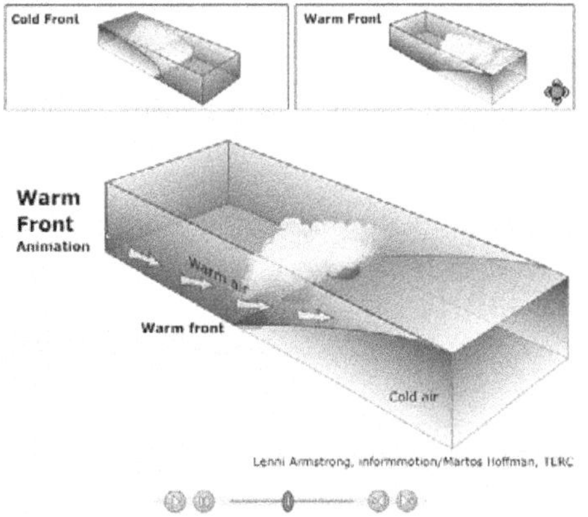

27) Observe a visual model of Earth's spheres.

http://www.classzone.com/books/earth_science/terc/content/visualizations/es0102/es0102page01.cfm

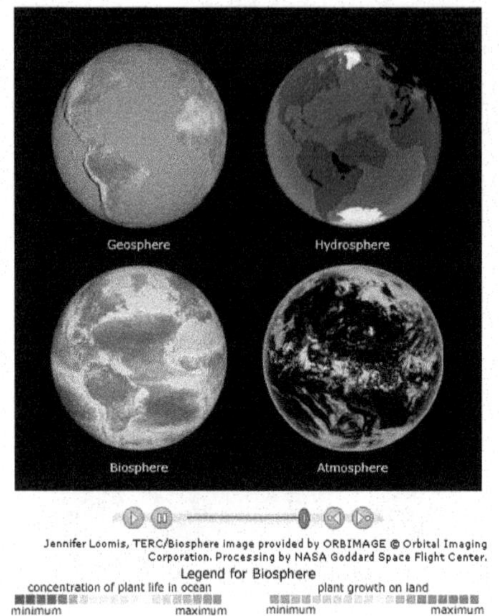

28) Experiment: Make Lightning!

The purpose of this experiment is to observe lightning formation.

Stuff you need

Styrofoam plate

Thumbtack

Pencil with new eraser

Aluminum pie pan

Small piece of wool fabric

Make it happen

1. Push the thumbtack through the center of the aluminum pie pan from the bottom.

2. Push the eraser end of the pencil into the thumbtack. (The pencil becomes a handle to lift the pan.)

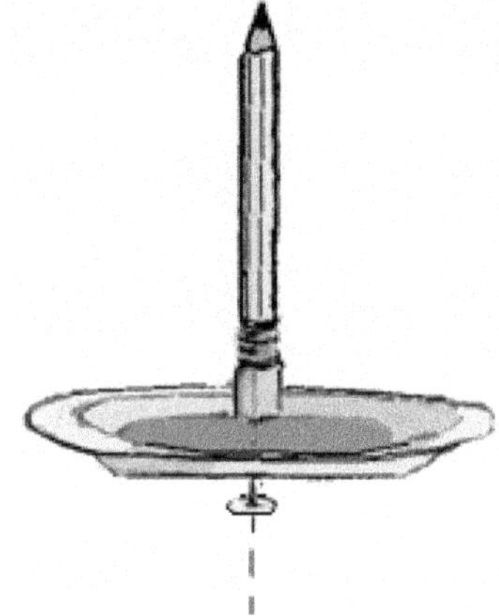

4. Put the styrofoam plate upside-down on a table. Rub the underside of the plate with the wool for one minute. Rub hard and fast.

4. Pick up the pie pan using the pencil "handle ", and place it on top of the upside-down plate.

5. Touch the pie pan with your finger. If you don't feel anything when you touch the pan, try rubbing the plate again.

Try turning the lights out before touching the pan. Do you see anything when you touch the pan?

29) Experiment: How far away is that storm?

The purpose of this experiment is **to watch lightning and hear thunder** to give you clues about **how far away you are from a storm**.

Stuff you need

One thunderstorm

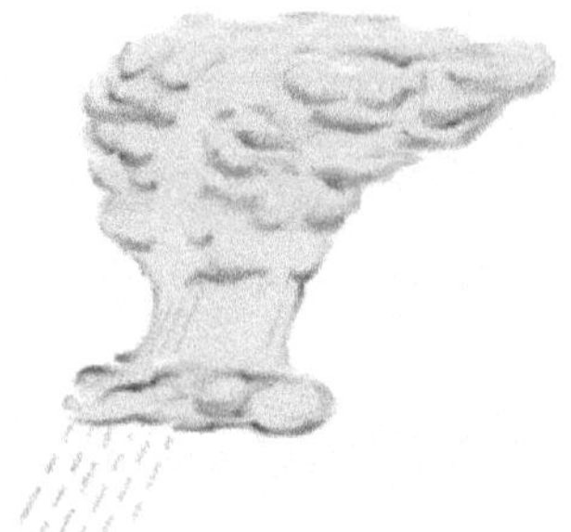

A stop watch (or the ability to say "one-Mississippi")

Make it happen

1. After you see a flash of lightning, count the number of seconds until you hear the thunder. (**Use the stop watch or count "One-Mississippi, Two-Mississippi, Three-Mississippi," etc.**)

2. For every 5 seconds the storm is one mile away. Divide the number of seconds you count by 5 to get the number of miles (one mille = 1.6 km)

What travels more quickly, light or sound?

If you said light travels faster than sound, you're right!

30) Experiment: Make Fog in a Jar!

Fog is a cloud that touches the ground or the surface of a body of water.

Stuff you need

Black paper

Matches

A jar (3 litres)

A bag of ice

Make it happen

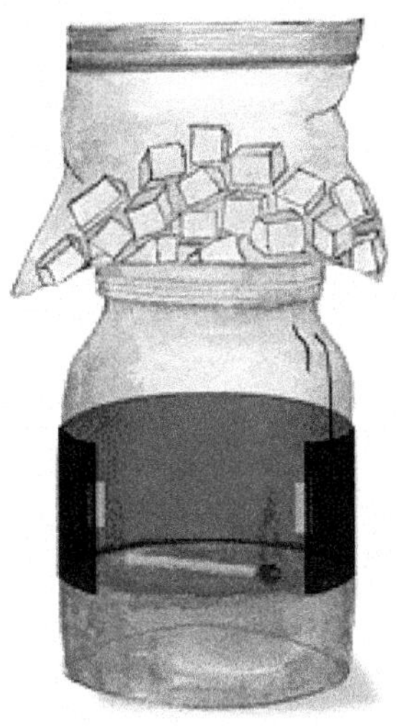

1. Tape the black paper on the back of the jar, so you can't see through the jar.

2. Fill one third of the jar with colored warm water.

3. Light the match and hold it over the jar opening.

4. After a few seconds, drop the match into the jar and cover the top of the jar with the bag of ice.

5. Record your observations.

Can you see anything happening inside the jar?

You should see a little cloud form.

The warm water heats the layer of air that it touches. Some of the water evaporates into the air forming water vapor. The warm air containing water vapor rises, and then cools, as it comes in contact with the air cooled by the ice. When the water molecules cool, they slow down and stick together more readily. The particles of smoke act as nuclei for "bunches" of water molecules to collect on. This process is called condensation.

2. THE HYDROSPHERE: LIQUID IN EARTH

ACTIVITIES

1) Read.

The hydrosphere is the mass of water that covers the Earth. The water of the hydrosphere forms:

OCEANS. They are big masses of **salty water**. The seas are parts of the oceans that have their own name.

RIVERS. They are currentes of **fresh water.**

LAKES. They are masses of fresh water.

SUBTERRANEAN CURRENTS. They go under the surface and come out at some points, forming fountains, springs wells, etc.

ICE and SNOW. They form big deposits of water in the poles and on the summits of the mountains.

2) Look and read. The hydrosphere.

All the water on Earth makes up the hydrosphere. Water is usually a liquid, but it can also be a solid or a gas.

Water in **liquid** form covers most of the Earth's surface. It is found in oceans, seas, rivers and lakes. Water in **solid** form (snow and ice) is found in the polar regions. It is also found on mountains. Water vapour, a **gas**, is found in the atmosphere.

Water can be a liquid or a solid, such as ice or snow.
Water vapour is in the atmosphere.

3) Read and color. The Water Cycle.

The sun heats up water on land and in the oceans, lakes, and seas. The water changes from liquid to vapor in a process called evaporation. The water vapor cools and in a process called condensation forms droplets in the atmosphere. These droplets become clouds. The droplets (or ice crystals) gather and then fall from the sky in a process called precipitation. This precipitation gathers in streams and rivers and flows and becomes run off, flowing back down to the oceans, seas, and lakes.

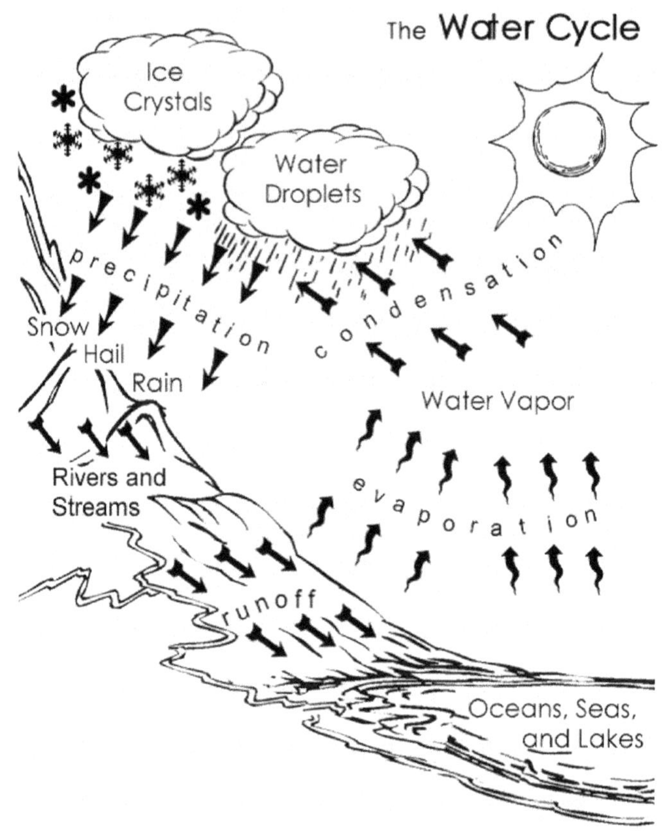

4) Read. The Water Cycle.

The **water cycle** is the constant circulation of water between the sea, the atmosphere and land.

1. Liquid water in the sea, rivers and lakes **evaporates** because of heat from the Sun. It becomes water vapour.

2. Water vapour rises and **condenses** into drops of water. The water drops form clouds.

3. Water falls from clouds as rain: **precipitation.** If it is very cold, water **solidifies** and falls as snow.

4. Water flows over the land and filters into it. It forms rivers and lakes.

Some water returns to the sea or **evaporates.** ***The water cycle starts again.***

5) Water Cycle mini-test.

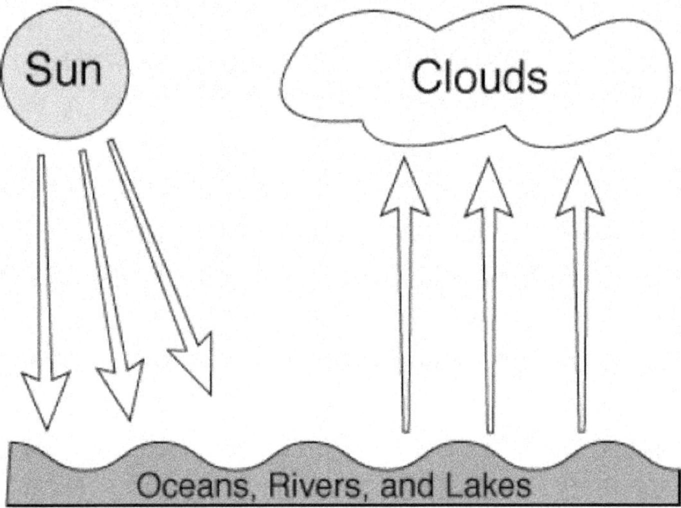

1. What is the name for water in solid form?

2. What is the name for water in liquid form?

3. What is the name for water in gaseous form?

4. Water covers _________% of the earth's surface and is vital to all living things.

5. When it becomes very hot outside, raindrops (evaporate, condense, precipitate).

6. When evaporated water forms into a cloud we call it (precipitation, condensation).

7. When water falls from the sky in the form of rain, snow, or sleet it is called (evaporation, condensation, precipitation).

6) **Water Cycle Word Search.**

M	V	R	A	P	E	J	N	S	T	R	J	L	F	P	M
G	L	I	P	H	W	V	I	B	Y	A	Q	A	F	U	L
C	N	V	R	A	A	T	A	A	C	D	N	K	O	A	W
V	U	E	E	I	T	Q	G	P	G	W	N	E	T	Z	P
L	W	R	C	L	E	E	Z	J	O	N	M	S	D	M	P
F	A	H	I	C	R	W	T	N	M	R	Y	B	D	N	F
O	T	E	P	T	D	T	S	B	A	R	A	K	Q	F	Z
C	E	V	I	B	R	Y	R	M	C	C	O	T	Z	S	S
E	R	W	T	C	O	N	D	E	N	S	A	T	I	O	N
A	V	A	A	L	P	T	C	C	L	Y	C	Q	H	O	E
N	A	B	T	T	L	I	P	S	G	X	L	K	T	E	N
W	P	B	I	C	E	B	J	R	I	Q	O	O	J	R	B
F	O	M	O	Q	T	R	E	J	O	G	U	U	M	A	R
D	R	O	N	Y	T	N	C	J	W	F	D	A	I	I	U
W	Q	T	H	N	E	V	W	Y	N	H	E	W	Z	N	N
T	I	F	E	R	W	I	H	U	C	R	M	N	L	I	O
W	D	N	S	E	A	J	S	K	T	L	R	N	G	Z	F
X	H	Q	D	Q	Y	M	J	S	H	W	E	D	F	P	F

cloud	ocean	stream
condensation	precipitation	sun
energy	rain	water cycle
evaporation	river	water droplet
hail	runoff	water vapor
ice crystal	sea	wind
lake	snow	

7) **Use the diagram to identify the different parts of the water cycle.**

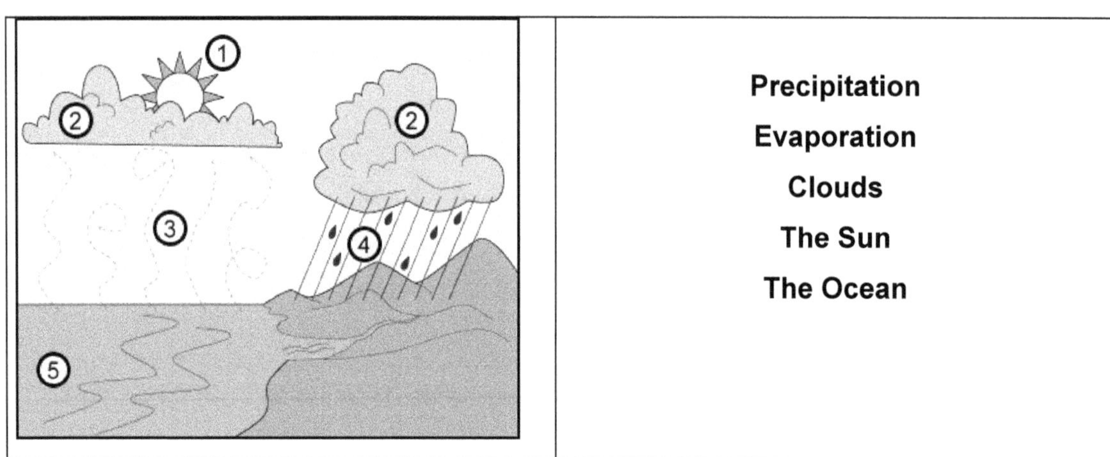

8) **Use the diagram to identify the different parts of the water cycle (II).**

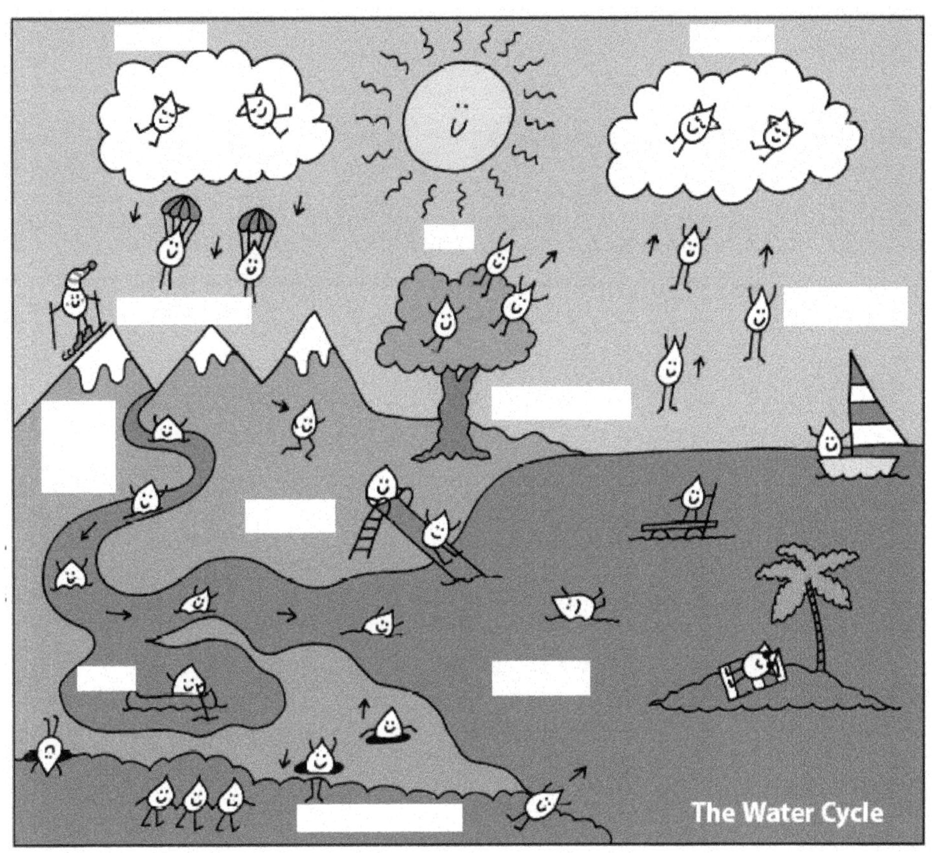

Clouds	Transpiration	Runoff
Sun	Ocean	Lake
Evaporation	Ground Water	

9) **Unscramble the letters.**

10) Read and color. The Drinking Water.

Drinking water comes from lakes, rivers, streams, or under the ground (ground water).

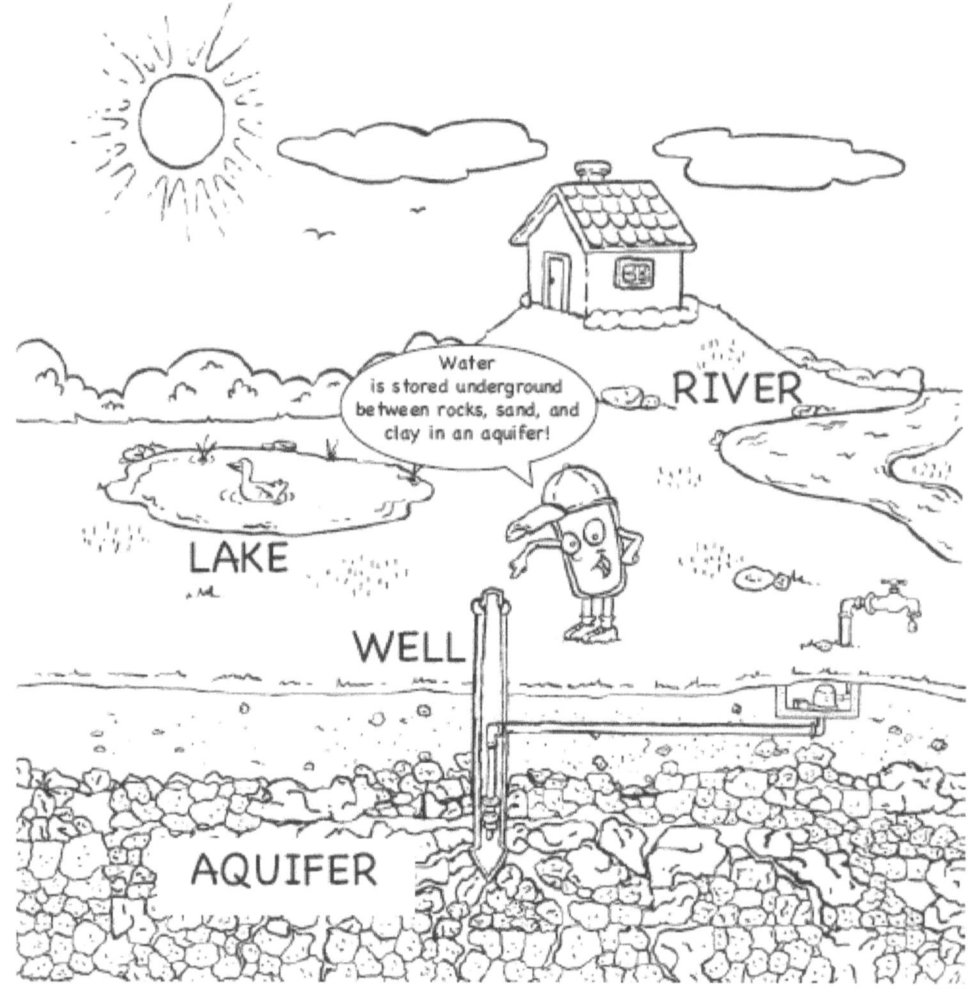

11) Because we need water to live, it is important to conserve as much water as we can.

You can help turning off the water when you're not using.

12) Think about.

1. How much water does it take to cook a Hamburger?

2. How long can a person live without food?

3. How long can a person live without water?

4. How much water is used to flush a toilet?

5. How much water is used to brush your teeth?

6. How much water does an individual use daily?

13) Choose the right option.

1. Where is most water found on Earth?
   A. in glaciers
   B. in lakes
   C. in rivers
   D. in oceans
2. What source of energy evaporates the most water from Earth's surface?
   A. volcanoes
   B. the sun
   C. lightning
   D. wind
3. What is water doing when it is changed to water vapor?
   A. evaporating
   B. condensing
   C. precipitating
   D. freezing
4. What is water vapor doing when it changes to water?
   A. evaporating
   B. condensing
   C. precipitating
   D. freezing

14) Use this model of the water cycle to answer the next three questions.

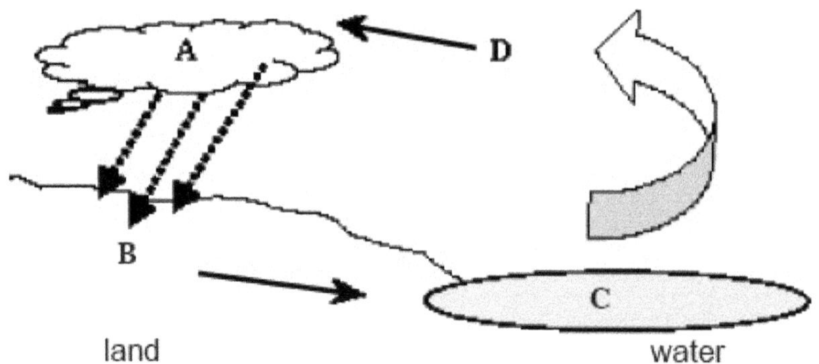

1. Where is water evaporating into the air?
   A. from A to B
   B. from B to C
   C. from C to D
   D. from D to A
2. Where is water condensing?
   A. from A to B
   B. from B to C
   C. from C to D
   D. from D to A
3. Where is precipitation occurring?
   A. from A to B
   B. from B to C
   C. from C to D
   D. from D to A

15) The Water Cycle.

http://www.epa.gov/safewater/kids/flash/flash_watercycle.html

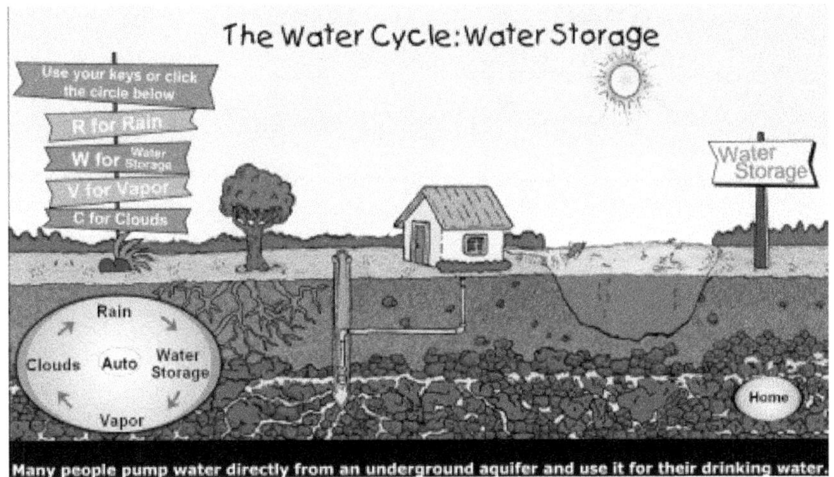

16) Learn about the Water Cycle.

http://www.sweetwater.org/education/watercycle.html

17) Interactive Word Scramble Game

http://www.epa.gov/safewater/kids/flash/flash_wordscramble.html

18) Water cycle diagram.

http://earthguide.ucsd.edu/earthguide/diagrams/watercycle/index.html

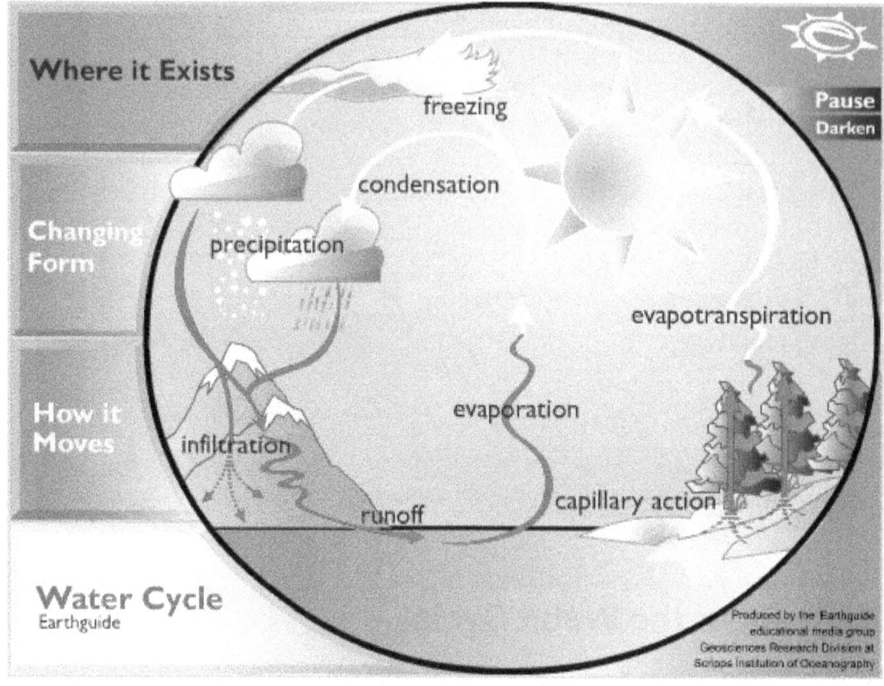

19) Water cycle quiz.

http://earthguide.ucsd.edu/earthguide/diagrams/watercycle/watercycleq.html

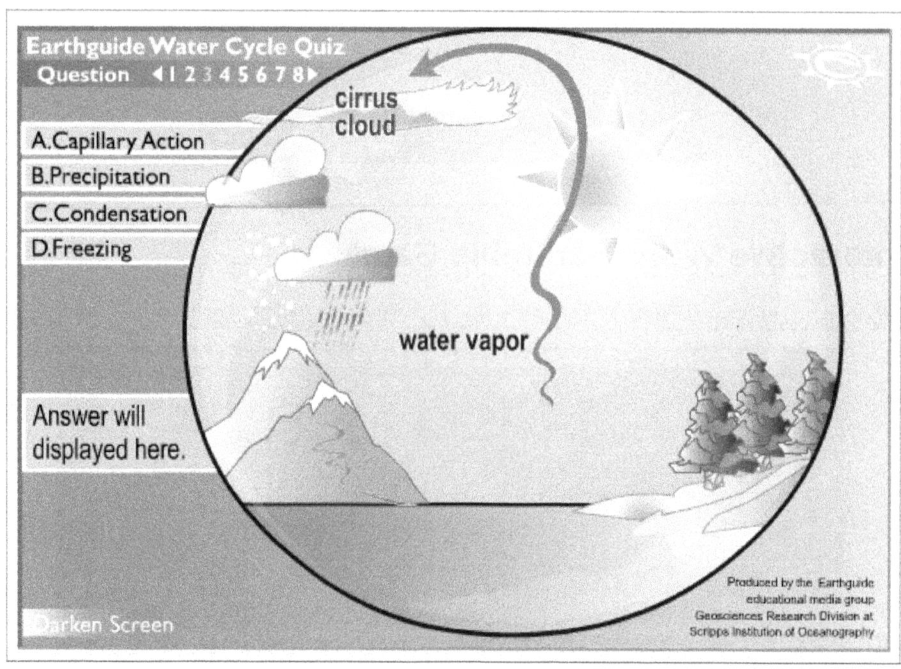

3. THE GEOSPHERE: THE SOLID PART OF EARTH. MINERALS AND ROCKS

ACTIVITIES

1) Read. The geosphere.

The **geosphere** is made up of three layers:

- The **crust** is the Earth's outer layer. It is made up of solid materials.
- The **mantle** is the Earth's middle layer. It is extremely hot. In some parts, there is **magma** (red-hot liquid rock).
- The **core** is the Earth's inner layer. It is also extremely hot. It is divided into the liquid outer core and the solid inner core.

2) Read the definitions and label the Earth Diagram.

Definitions

- **Crust**: the rigid, rocky outer surface of the Earth, composed mostly of basalt and granite. The crust is thinner under the oceans.
- **Inner core:** the solid iron-nickel center of the Earth that is very hot and under great pressure.
- **Mantle**: a rocky layer located under the crust (it is composed of silicon, oxygen, magnesium, iron, aluminum, and calcium). Convection (heat) currents carry heat from the hot inner mantle to the cooler outer mantle.
- **Outer core**: the molten iron-nickel layer that surrounds the inner core.

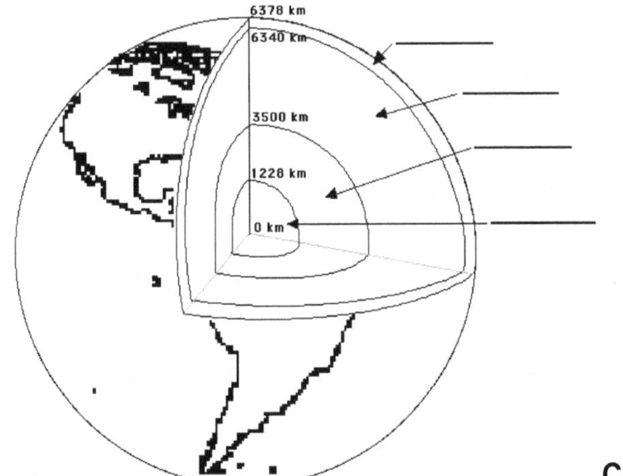

Color it

3) Layers of Earth.

Label the three layers of Earth. Then write 2 interesting facts about each layer.

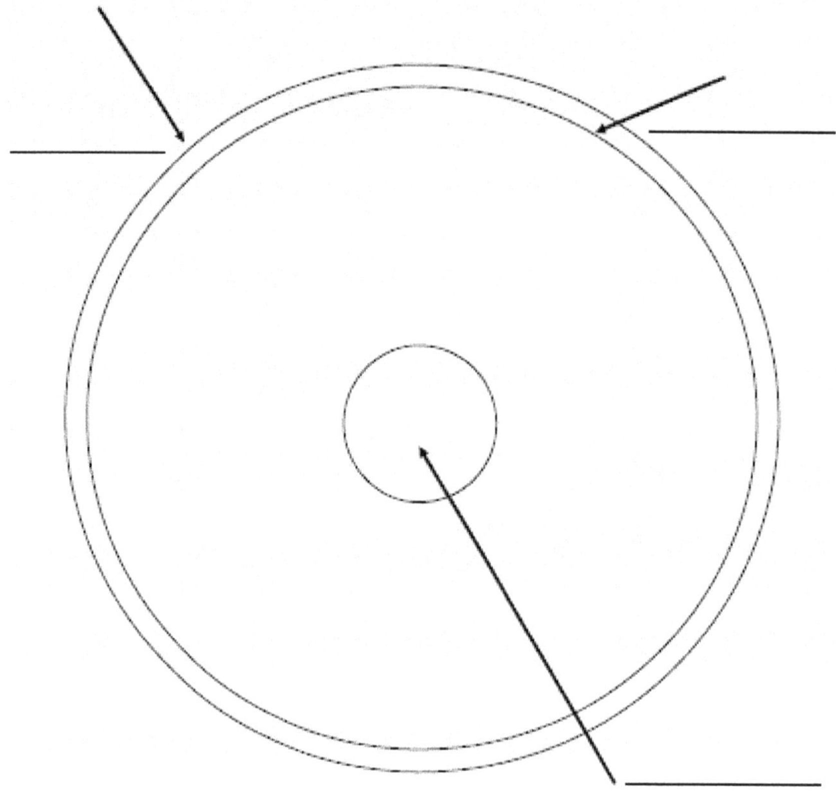

4) Read. Rocks and minerals.

Rocks are natural materials which make up the Earth's crust.

Rocks are made up of minerals. Minerals are pure. We cannot break them down into other substance. There are hundreds of minerals, such as diamond and other precious stones. We can identify each mineral by its density, colour, hardness and shine.

5) Read. Types of rock.

Rocks can be classified into three types depending on how they are formed:

- **Sedimentary rocks** are formed from pieces of other rocks or pieces of living things. Coal and gypsum are sedimentary rocks.
- **Igneous rocks** are formed when magma cools ar solidifies. Granite and basalt are igneous rocks.
- **Metamorphic rocks** are formed when heat.

6) The rock cycle. "turns in to".

It is similar to the water cycle, but uses rocks. When reading this chart the arrows are read like **"turns in to."** For example: Igneous rock turns in to sediment (because of weathering and erosion).

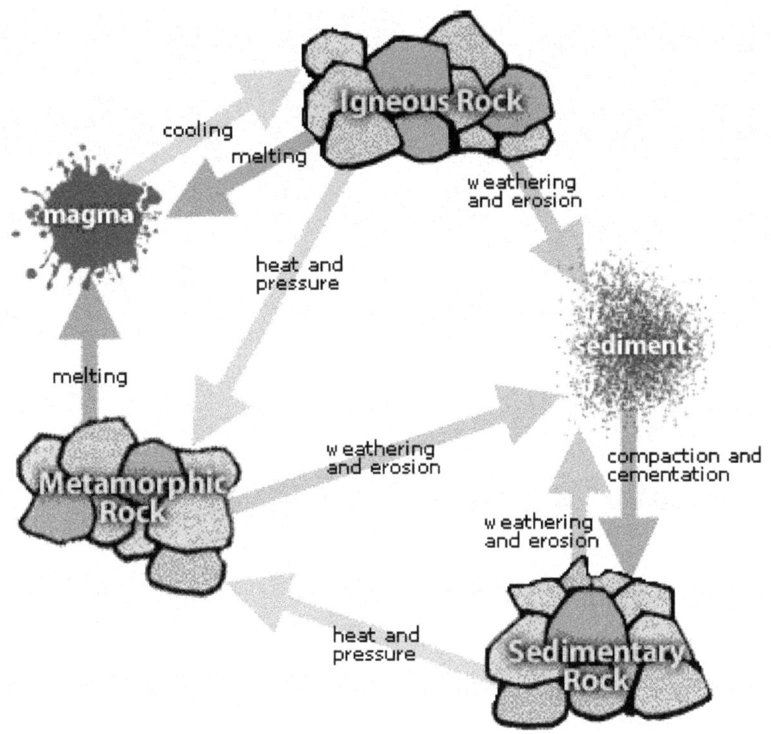

7) Complete the table by ticking the appropriate statements.

The three kinds of rocks.

statement	igneous	sedimentary	metamorphic
a. formed from molten lava or magma	✓		
b. formed by the action of heat and pressure			
c. formed when substances settle in water and are compressed over millions of years			
d. sandstone is an example			
e. basalt is an example			
f. limestone is an example			
g. granite is an example			
h. slate is an example			

statement	igneous	sedimentary	metamorphic
i. marble is an example			
j. pumice is an example			
k. often contain fossils			
l. have small crystals when they cool quickly			

8) Complete the diagram by adding labels in the correct place. The rock cycle.

Use words from this list:

grains compact and stick together

weathering & erosion *(used twice)*

heat & pressure

cooling & crystallisation

melting

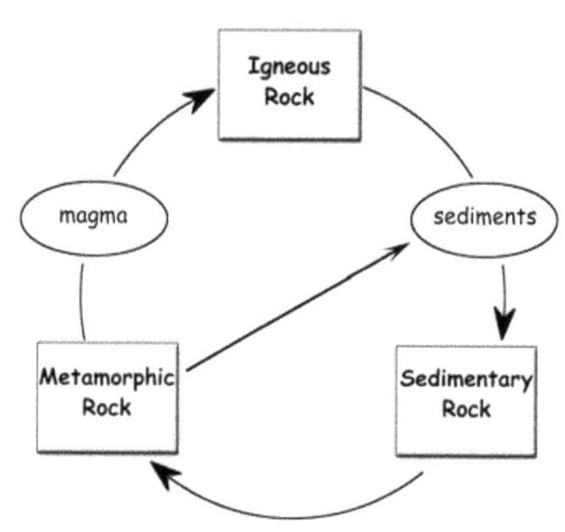

9) Join with arrows.

1. A naturally occurring, nonliving solid with a definite structure and composition	**a.** rock
2. A mixture of minerals, mineraloids, glass, or organic matter	**b.** mineral
3. Processes by which rocks form and change	**c.** quartz
4. A hard silicate mineral	**d.** granite
5. An igneous rock made up of mica, feldspar, quartz.	**e.** rock cycle

10) Read. "Weathering".

The action of wind and water is called **weathering:**

- **Erosion** is the removal of soil and rocks by wind and water. For example, the sea's waves gradually erode a cliff.
- **Transport** is the movement of eroded material. For example, rivers, seas and the wind carry sand.
- **Sedimentation** is the accumulation of eroded material from other places. For example, mud settles at the bottom of a river.

11) Write each word in the box under the correct heading.

weathering	igneous	melting	cooling
erosion	sedimentary	compaction	cementation
deposition	heating	metamorphic	

Processes in the rock cycle	Kinds of rocks

12) Complete each sentence.

a) Erosion is the removal of rocks by ____________________

-volcanic activity -wind and water

b) Transport is the ______________________ of eroded material.

-movement -eruption

c) Sedimentation is the ______________________ of eroded material.

-destruction -accumulation

13) Read. "Volcanoes".

Volcanoes form in places where there is **magma** (red-hot liquid rock) just under the surface. When a volcano erupts, internal forces push the magma up through a central pipe, thevolcanic **chimney.** It emerges through a circular opening called a **crater.** Magma is called **lava** when it reaches the Earth's surface. Lava moves down, destroying everything in its path. Layers of lava form a volcanic **cone.**

14) Read. Parts of a Volcano.

Volcanoes are mountains that have hot lava and magma inside. Below the Earth's crust is a solid body of rock called the mantle. Pressure and extrememly high temperatures melt the rock. This melted rock is called **magma**. Magma is stored in a **magma chamber**. The magma pushes up to the Earth's crust through a conduit or **pipe** in the volcano. It can also branch off to side vents and create parasitic cones. When the magma reaches the surface it is called lava.

Lava comes through the main vent when the volcano erupts. This can create a **crater** at the top of the volcano. Lava flows down the **side or flank** of the volcano. When the lava cools, it turns into rock. Each eruption creates another layer of rock that builds up the volcano.

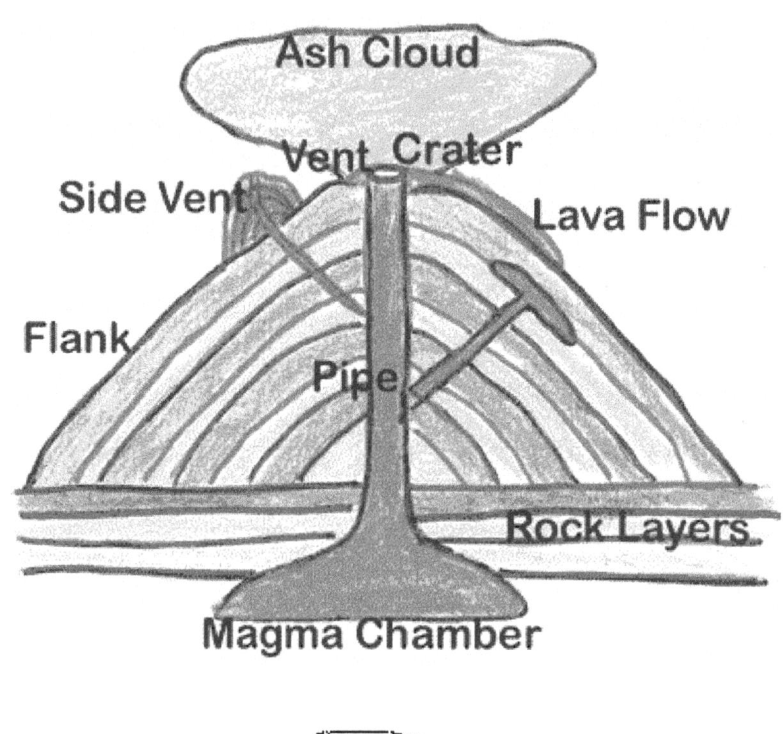

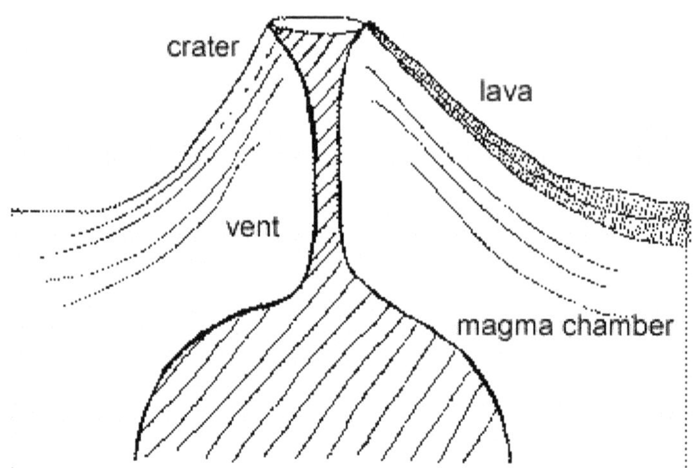

15) Color and label the Volcano Diagram. Use the words in the box.

ash cloud	conduit	crust	lava
magma chamber	side vent	vent	

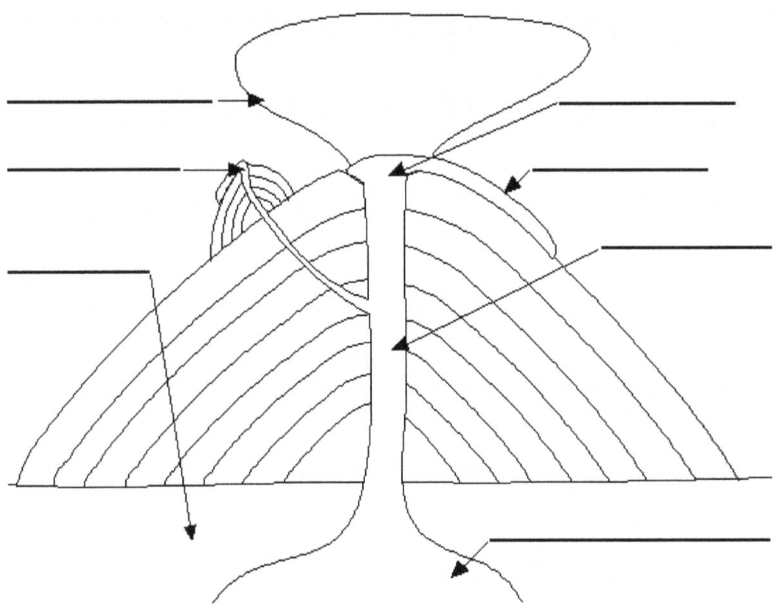

16) Read. "Earthquakes".

Earthquakes are caused by movements of the firth's crust. They can destroy buildings and idges, divert rivers, and cause avalanches. Earthquakes on the ocean floor produce enormous, destructive waves called tsunamis.

17) Color the volcano.

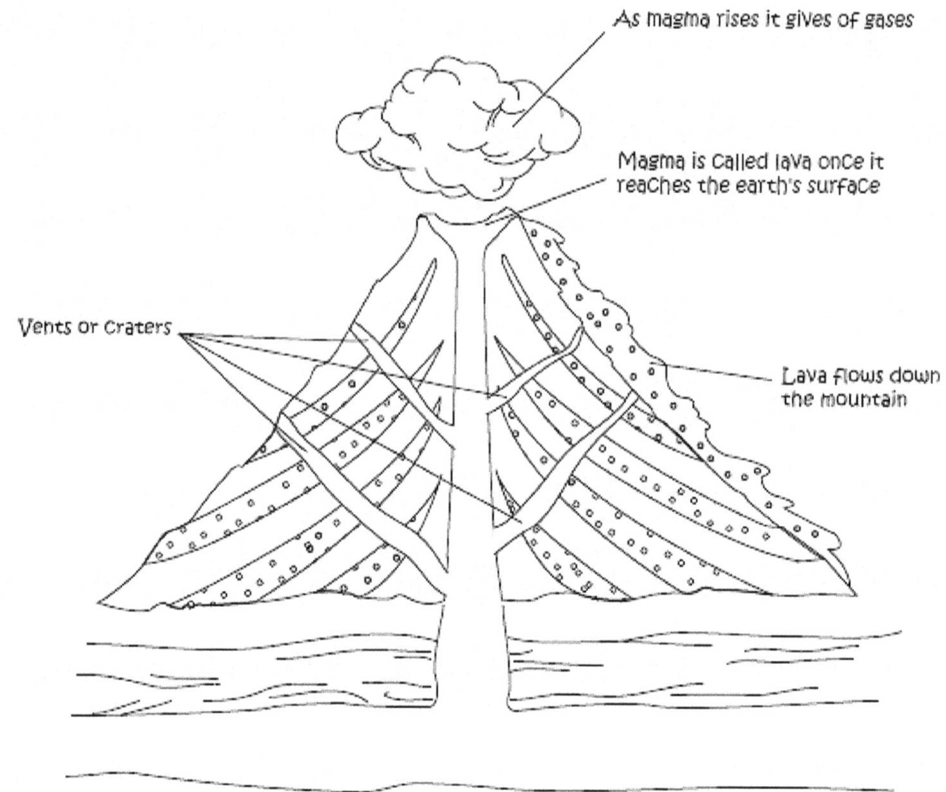

18) Color and label Earth.

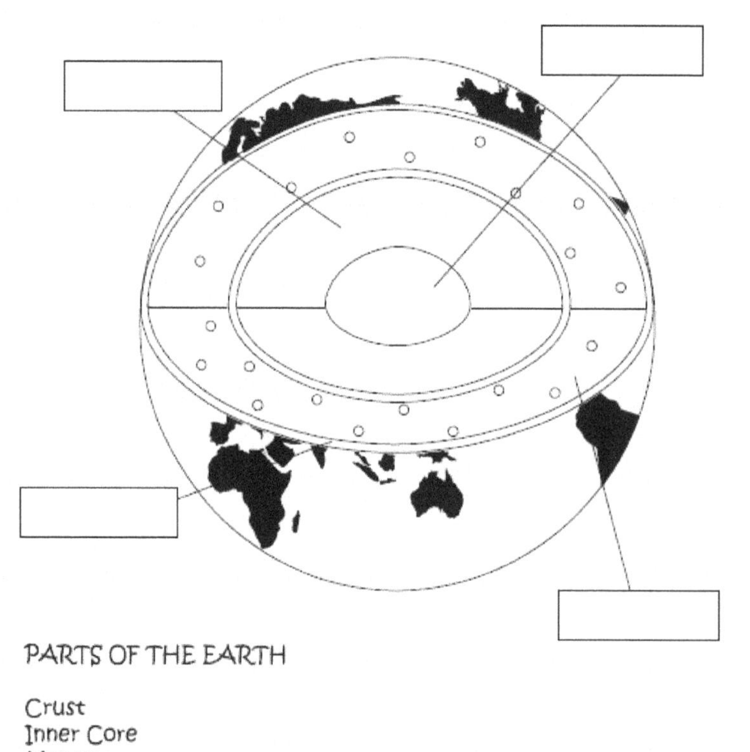

PARTS OF THE EARTH

Crust
Inner Core
Mantle
Outer Core

19) Observe how sediments are deposited.

http://www.classzone.com/books/earth_science/terc/content/visualizations/es0604/es0604page01.cfm

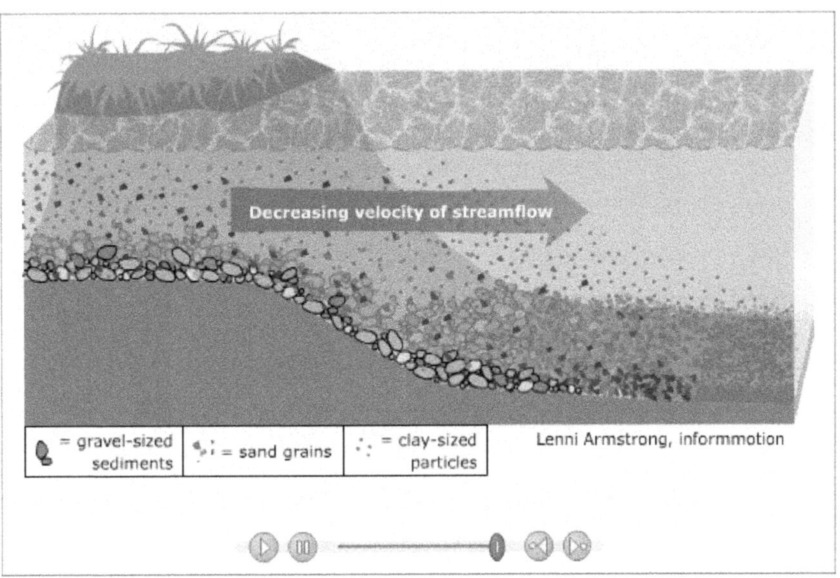

20) Observe an animation of sedimentary rocks forming.

http://www.classzone.com/books/earth_science/terc/content/visualizations/es0605/es0605page01.cfm

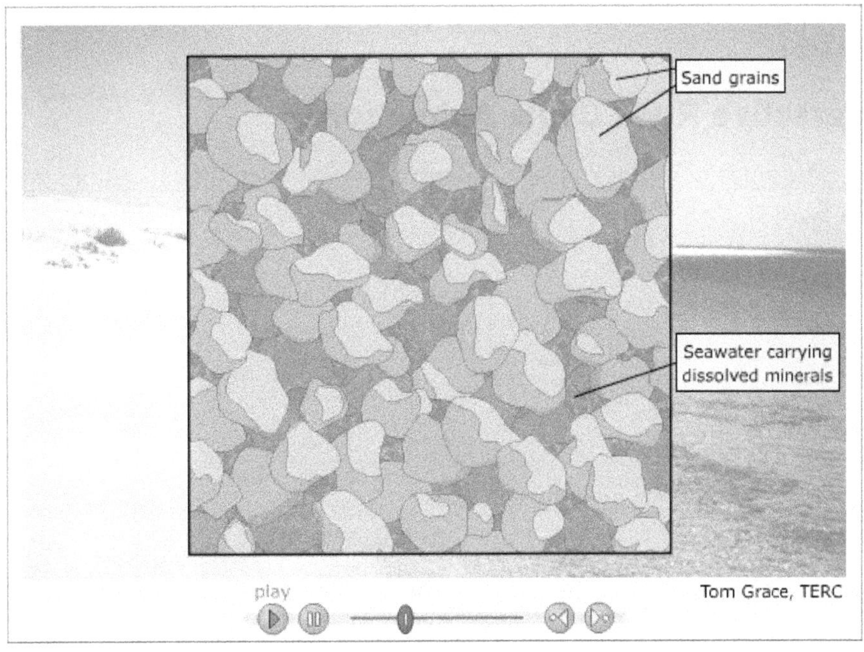

21) Animated guide: Volcanoes.

http://news.bbc.co.uk/2/hi/science/nature/4972366.stm

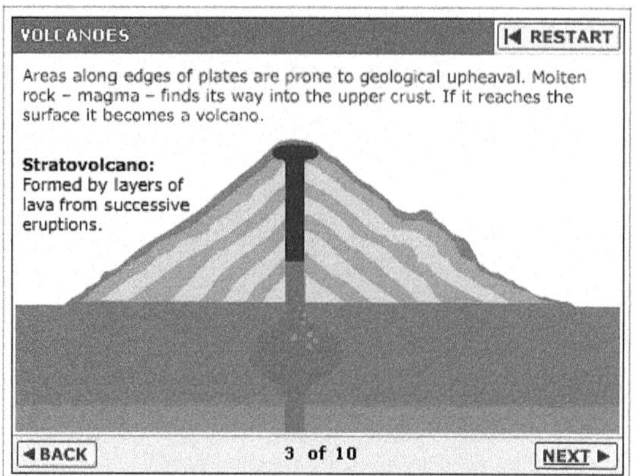

22) Tsunami explained.

http://news.bbc.co.uk/2/hi/asia-pacific/5194316.stm

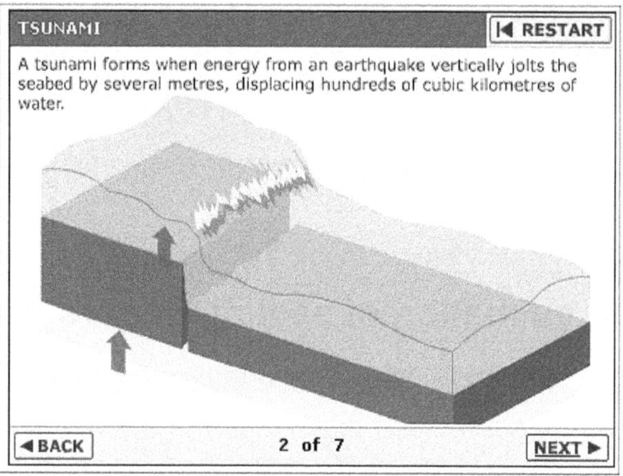

23) Interactive Rock Cycle Animation.

http://www.classzone.com/books/earth_science/terc/content/investigations/es0602/es0602page02.cfm

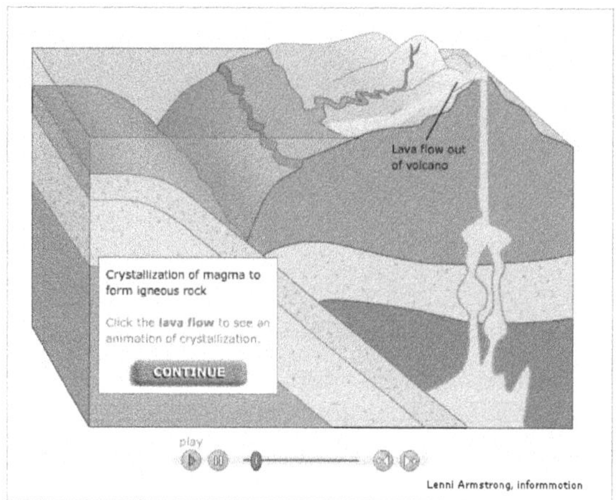

24) Rock Cycle Diagram.

http://www.classzone.com/books/earth_science/terc/content/investigations/es0602/es0602page03.cfm

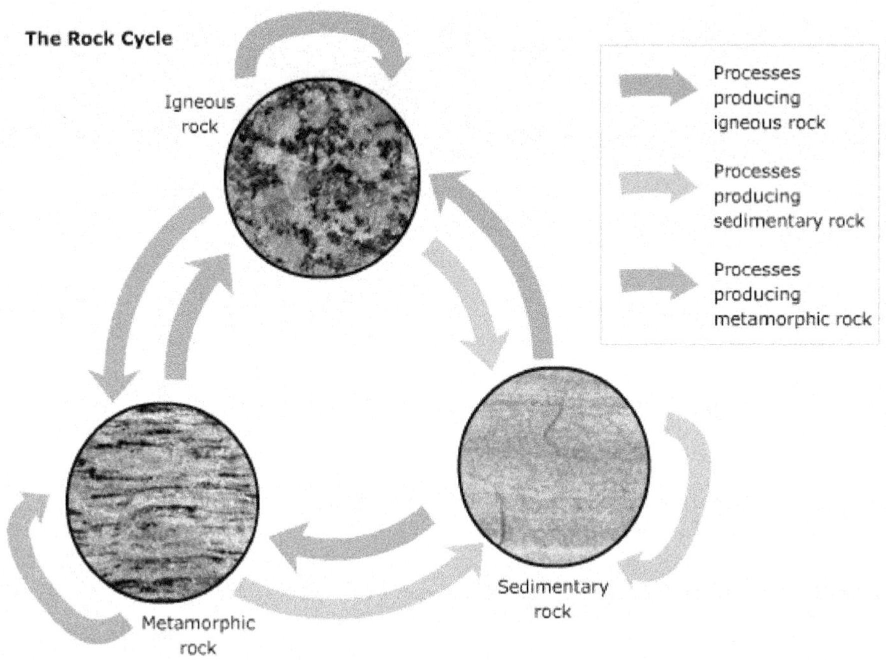

4. PROTECTING THE EARTH PLANET

ACTIVITIES

1) Human beings have an influence on the environment.

People are part of the biosphere. We don't usually use natural resources properly and we don't care about the negative effects that we can produce.

ACTIONS AGAINST THE ENVIRONMENT

Air pollution:

Cars and the industry pollute the air. This pollution causes respiratory problems and destroys plants.

Water pollution:

Water is polluted because we throw waste substances into the rivers and the sea. When this happens there is less drinking water, we cannot swim in the sea or in the rivers, and some species die.

Deforestation:

We cut trees to have wood and lands to grow vegetables. When we do this, we do harm to the living creatures that live'in the forest and the climate changes. The land becomes a desert and many plants and animals disappear.

Destruction of the ozone layer:

The ozone layer is essential to live because it protects us from the harmful beams of the sun. Some chemical products that we use destroy the ozone layer and now there is a hole in the ozone layer above the Antarctica.

DIFFERENT WAYS TO PROTECT THE ENVIRONMENT

Reduction of pollution

We have to use the public transports and use the energy correctly.

Planting trees in deforested areas

We don't have to cut more trees and that is why we have to recycle paper.

Maintaining protected species and protected areas

We can do this if we don't buy ivory objects, fur coats, etc.

Reducing the quantity of rubbish and recycling things that we use.

2) Think about and answer the questions

1) Write three actions that you can do to protect an ecosystem.

2) Say whether these sentsnces are TRUE or FALSE.

- ❑ Deforestation is the loss of forest and green areas.
- ❑ Planting new trees is not good for the ecosystems.
- ❑ The land becomes a desert when the fertile soil becomes sterile.
- ❑ If you recycle rubbish you produce more rubbish.

3) Write the name of some animals and plants that are protected in Spain.

3) Read. The ozone Layer (I).

The ozone layer forms a thin shield high up in the sky. It protects life on Earth from the sun's ultraviolet (UV) rays. In the 1980s, scientists began finding clues that the ozone layer being depleted. This allows more UV radiation to reach the Earth's surface. This can cause people to have a greater chance of getting too much UV radiation. Too much UV can cause bad health effects like skin cancer or eye damage.

What is Stratospheric Ozone?

Ozone is a natural gas that is found in the stratosphere layer. Ozone protects life on Earth by absorbing some of the sun's UV rays. Stratospheric ozone is found most often between six to 30 miles above the Earth's surface.

4) Read. The ozone Layer (II).

The **ozone layer** is very important because it stops too many of the sun's 'ultra-violet rays' (UV rays) getting through to the Earth - these are the rays that cause our skin to tan. **Too much UV** can cause **skin cancer** and will also harm all plants and animals. **Life on Earth could not exist without the protective shield of the ozone layer.**

WHAT IS THE OZONE HOLE?

Every spring, a hole as big as the USA develops in the ozone layer over Antarctica, in the South Pole. A smaller hole develops each year over the Arctic, at the North Pole. The loss of the ozone layer occurs when more ozone is being destroyed than nature is creating.

5) Read. What causes the ozone hole?

One group of gases is particularly likely to damage the ozone layer. These gases are called CFCs, Chloro-Fluoro-Carbons.

CFCs are used in some spray. They are also used in **refrigerators**, **air conditioning systems** and some **fire extinguishers**.

6) Read. The ozone hole and our health.

The ozone layer is like a **sunscreen**. Too many UV rays would cause more **sunburn**, and because sunburn causes **skin cancer**, this too would increase deaths.
These UV rays are also **dangerous for our eyes**. Sun **cream and sunglasses** are very important.

7) Each of the following five questions has one correct answer. Do you know what it is?

1. WHERE IS THE OZONE LAYER?
   - ❑ Between 5 and 10 km.
   - ❑ Between 15 and 35 km.
   - ❑ Between 50 and 100 km.
2. WHY IS THE OZONE LAYER CALLED A PROTECTIVE LAYER?
   - ❑ It protects the sun.
   - ❑ It protects the ozone.
   - ❑ It protects the Earth.
3. WHICH OF THE FOLLOWING PRODUCTS CONTAIN CFCs?
   - ❑ Televisions.
   - ❑ Ovens.
   - ❑ Refrigerators.
4. SKIN CANCER, EYE CATARACTS AND CROP DAMAGE MAY ALL BE CAUSED BY WHAT?
   - ❑ The tides.
   - ❑ An expanding ozone layer.
   - ❑ A thinning ozone layer.

6. COUNTRIES NOT PRODUCING CFCs WILL NOT BE AFFECTED BY HOLES IN THE OZONE LAYER.

   True | False

8) The Earth's atmosphere and its layers.

Ozone in the ozone layer protects us against the dangerous ultra-violet radiation from the Sun. Ozone absorbs the ultra-violet radiation.

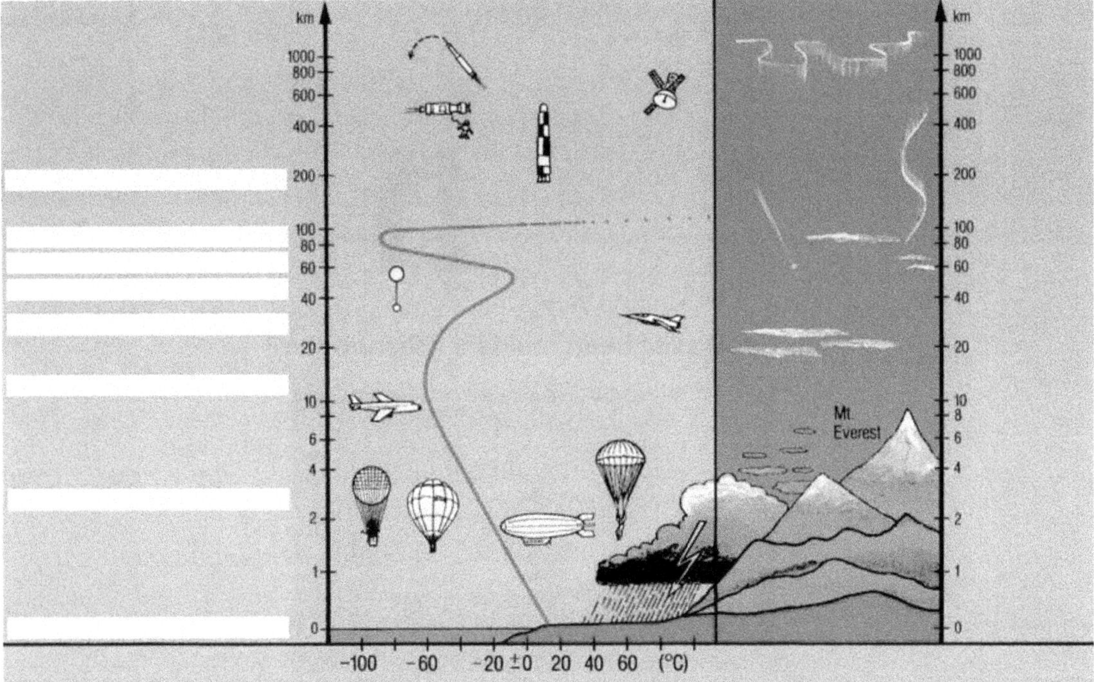

a) Fill in the white boxes with the words: **mesosphere, troposphere, sea level, stratosphere, stratopause, thermosphere, mesopause, tropopause.**

b) Draw on the position of the ozone layer.

9) Read. The Greenhouse Effect.

The greenhouse effect is the **rise in temperature** that the Earth experiences because certain gases in the atmosphere **(water vapor, carbon dioxide, nitrous oxide, and methane**) trap energy from the sun.

Greenhouses are used to grow plants, especially in the winter. Greenhouses work by trapping heat from the sun.

The Earth's atmosphere is all around us. It is the air that we breathe. Greenhouse gases in the atmosphere behave much like the glass panes in a greenhouse.

10) What causes the greenhouse effect?

Have you ever been inside a greenhouse?

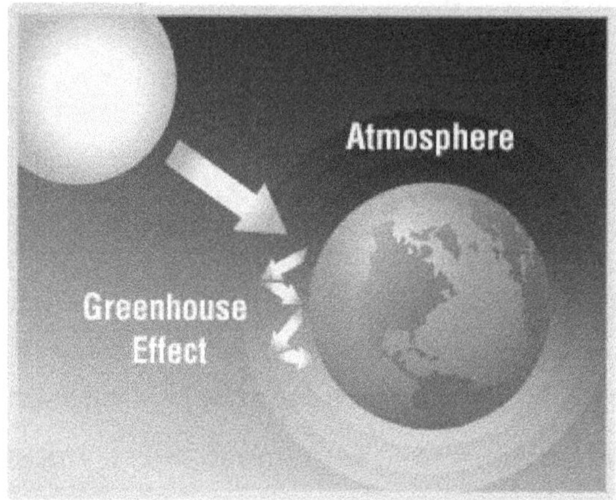

Greenhouse gases:

- Water vapour
- Carbon dioxide
- Methane
- Nitrous oxide

The Earth's atmosphere naturally contains these greenhouse gases, over the past few decades their presence has increased, causing the temperature of the earth to increase. The following human activities are the biggest contributors to the increase of greenhouse gases:

- burning gasoline to drive cars and trucks
- burning oil, coal or wood to produce electricity for heating, cooling and other purposes
- burning forests to clear land

11) Choose the right option.

1. Greenhouses are used to help plants grow, generally in which season?
   - ❑ Spring
   - ❑ Summer
   - ❑ Autumn
   - ❑ Winter
2. There is only one gas that causes the greenhouse effect.
   - ❑ True
   - ❑ False
3. What's the name of the lower atmosphere that contains the greenhouse gases?
   - ❑ Stratosphere
   - ❑ It doesn't have a name.
   - ❑ It's just called the "atmosphere".
   - ❑ Troposphere
4. The greenhouse effect and ozone hole are not the same.
   - ❑ True
   - ❑ False
5. Which of these is NOT a greenhouse gas?
   - ❑ Methane
   - ❑ Water vapour
   - ❑ Carbon monoxide
   - ❑ Carbon dioxide

12) What is Global Warming?

Global warming means that the average temperature of earth is raising either naturally or through an increase in greenhouse gases.

13) How can we stop global warming?

There are even some things that you can do to help slow this process:

- Walk, ride your bicycle, or take the bus instead of always going by car.
- Don't waste electricity (turn off the lights, the radio, the TV and the computer when you're not using them).
- Remember the 3R's: reduce, reuse, and/or recycle all kinds of items.
- Plant trees to help absorb excess CO_2, and to provide shade.

14) Switch off!

For my health …

For your health …

For the planet's health …

For the health of your bank account…

Be Part of the P⊘lluti⊘n S⊘luti⊘n

15) **Coloring. Don't pollute!**

16) **Draw a line between each object and the appropriate bin where it should be placed.**

17) **Color. Recycling.**

18) **Color. Composting.**

19) The signing of my contract.

Every day we hear about **problems** with our **environment**.

We hear about **pollution**, **acid rain**, **global warming**, the **destruction of rainforests**, or the decline and **extinction of plants and animals**, there is one clear message: our environment is in trouble, and **we need to do anything**.

Most of the **problems** with our environment occur as a direct result of **human activity**.

Protecting the Earth Planet
I, ____,
pledge to do my part to take good care of our planet.
I will try to help by not wasting water, keeping our air clean,
and protecting our trees and plants.

20) Can or Cannot/Can't: Recycle, Compost or Garbage?

Look at the pictures and fill in the blanks with can or cannot/can't to complete each sentence.

Examples:

1. An apple ___*can*___ be composted. 
2. A pop can ___*cannot/can't*___ be composted.  
3. Tissues ________________ be recycled.  
4. Glass bottles ________________ be reused and recycled.  
5. Egg shells ________________ be composted.  
6. Banana peels ________________ be recycled.  
7. Pet hair ________________ only go in the garbage.  
8. Carrots ________________ be recycled.  
9. Candy wrappers ________________ only go in the garbage.   
10. Newspapers and paper ________________ be recycled.

Solutions. **can:** 1,4,5,7,9,10. **can't:** 2,3,6,8.

21) Animated diagram of the greenhouse effect.

http://earthguide.ucsd.edu/earthguide/diagrams/greenhouse/

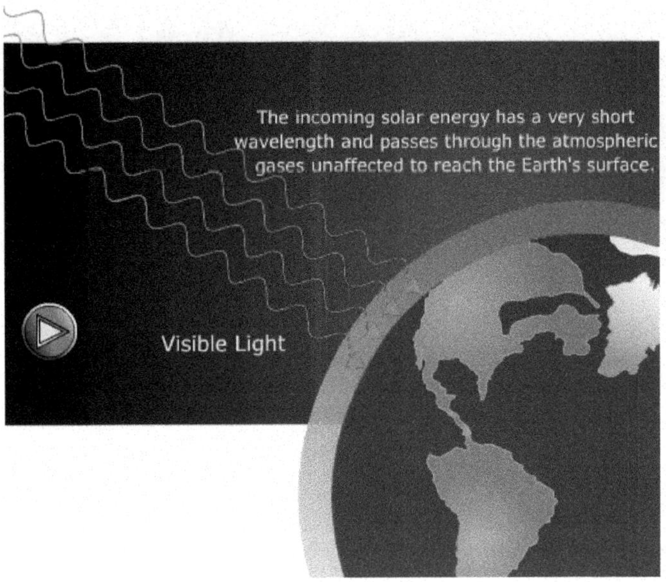

22) The Recycling Game.

http://www.bbc.co.uk/schools/barnabybear/games/recycle.shtml

23) Recycle Fun Game.

http://www.durham.gov.uk/kids/usp.nsf/pws/DCC+Kids+-+Games+-+Recycle+Fun

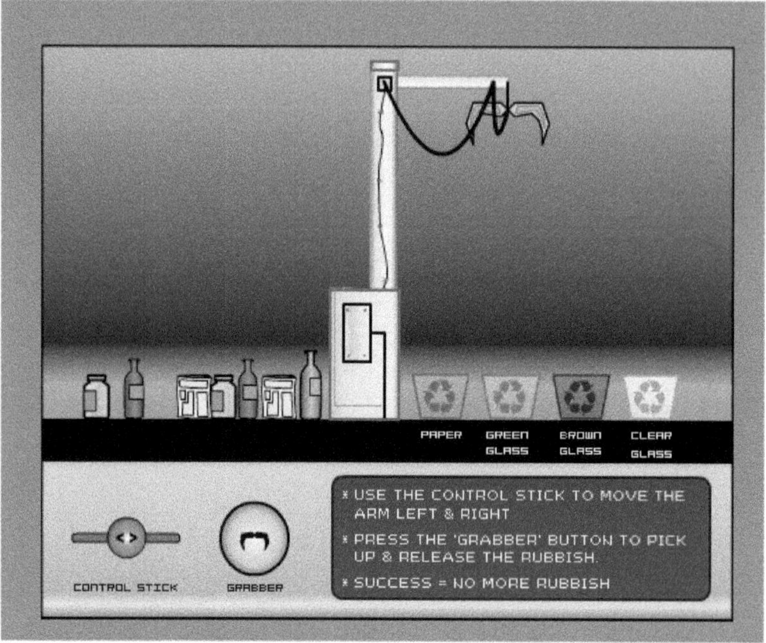

VOCABULARY AND NOTES

www.ingramcontent.com/pod-product-compliance
Ingram Content Group UK Ltd.
Pitfield, Milton Keynes, MK11 3LW, UK
UKHW050613260726
13967UKWH00008B/2847

9 781847 996169